The Book of Visions

with symbols drawn by

Curtis D. Yax

ISBN 978-1-64492-037-4 (paperback)
ISBN 978-1-64492-038-1 (digital)

Christian Faith Publishing
832 Park Avenue
Meadville, PA 16335
www.christianfaithpublishing.com

All scripture quotations taken from the King James Version

Printed in the United States of America

This book does not endorse or condemn any
denomination, sect, cult or religious organization.

Contents

List of Symbols

Christo seal (known symbols combined by the author). The XP monogram in the middle of the cross is an abbreviation for the first two letters of the Greek word for Christ (XPIETOE). The dove above the cross symbolizes the Holy Spirit. The cross was used in the execution of Jesus Christ.

Uniting these different symbols describes the Messiah's great commission—to take the place of the Sacrificial Lamb.

The Awakening Hymn

Chapter 1

Vision of Christ

This is a true testimony which I, Curtis D. Yax, witnessed concerning numerous, divine visions and prophecies given by God our Father, through the gifts of the Holy Spirit and Jesus Christ the Lord (Revelation 10:2–11).

The Word of God came to me, and I heard a voice from heaven say, "Awake, Curtis, awaken!" So like a jonquil breaking ground in the spring, my soul awoke. And I responded to the call—as an eye witness and Christian prophet, writing this book with the utmost care (Numbers 11:29).

I was in the Spirit and saw the Son of man with the clouds of heaven. His thick hair was long and black as coal, flowing over his shoulders. His features were handsome, like a young man's. And the Lord Jesus looked the same as he did two thousand years ago when he lived as a Jew in Israel (Revelation 1:7).

A glorious light shone in the back of him, lighting the clouds all about. He sat very meek, like a lamb and was full of grace. Everything was quite calm and very tranquil as I watched and patiently waited.

Then suddenly, Christ and the whole area around him began to lift up and went toward me. As it did, the Lord began to shine. His hair and beard turned white from the light, and so did his face and clothes (Daniel 7:9; Revelation 1:7, 14).

And then the light and glory behind him and from him began to radiate outward in all directions. As the glorified Son of God came nearer in a splendorous halo, the light grew exponentially in strength; his presence became majestic like a lion's (2 Peter 1:16–18; Revelation 1:14, 15).

When he went overhead, the dazzling light became so powerful and blinding that I thought I would die. So I was released from the glorious vision (Luke 21:27; Mark 14: 62).

Chapter 2

The Eucharist

Again, the Word came to me, and I received this fantastic vision: I saw myself in church, standing in line and waiting to receive Holy Communion. As I watched myself amid the congregation, I noticed that I looked older. The Catholic priest raised up the bread of life and blessed it. Then when the people came up to receive Holy Communion, I witnessed a remarkable occurrence.

When I took the Eucharist into my mouth, it immediately reached into my heart and soul. Rays of light began to emanate from my face, and like living waters, I could feel the power of God rushing through me (John 4:14; Revelation 11:3).

His glory began to consume my whole being. I could no longer see myself due to the blinding Christ light shining from me in all directions (Matthew 17:2; 1 John 3:2).

Like the vision of our Lord Jesus, the light became so terrifying and great that I thought I would perish. But again I was knocked out of the vision and could feel the awesome power of Jesus all night.

Then when I went to church, I saw that it was similar to the place in my night vision.

Often, while the priest prepared the Eucharist and during the transubstantiation, my body would tremble, being overwhelmed by the power of God. Moreover, the memory of our Lord's Last Supper caused me to weep uncontrollably. How forcefully the body of Christ rushed throughout my body! I was engulfed in the rhapsody! But after a while, a profound peace would come over me unlike anything I've experienced. I awoke and came into a new birth, a new life, a new consciousness, and a new reality (Luke 22:19, 20; Matthew 26:26–28).

Praise God that I returned to the Rock of Saint Peter, that the Lord Jesus called me back to the place of my baptism, the Holy Roman Catholic Church. For I was baptized there in 1952.

Let the Spirit of God be poured out in these final "last days," opening our minds and hearts to our Lord Jesus. Let us awaken!

Chapter 3

The Netherworld: Vision of Hell

Now on Sunday, June 23, 1974, I went to mass and received the Sacred Host. Later in the evening, I was raptured, and witnessed a most extraordinary vision from God.

I was lifted by the power of Christ and went through the clouds that separated before me. Mists surrounded me. With apparent ease, I passed through the clouds and went straight up, for my soul was transcendent (Ezekiel 8:1–3, 11:1, 24; Revelation 4:1, 2).

Above me, I saw three souls sent by Jesus, each surrounded by a protective globe-like sheath. I, too, was cloaked in an embryonic shield, which was oval and transparent. I followed them through the clouds, and we came high above the earth.

Advancing through the stratosphere to the heights of space, I briefly looked back and saw the earth. Like a musical sphere, it sang out with life (Habakkuk 3:3).

For a moment, we stopped, and seeing a man-made satellite, I went to examine it. But I was abruptly caught away by the Spirit and with unimaginable speed went past the moon into deep space.

Within minutes, I could see the mystifying rings of Saturn appear. The many brightly colored rings engirdled the golden planet, and I saw the flattened polar regions on top as I marveled when we went by (Acts 8:39, 40).

We continued the course, exceeding the speed of light, piercing through the fabric of space-time, passing other worlds swaddled with iridescent clouds. Their splendor was exquisite, and I gave thought to how magnificent God's creations are. How graceful are the works of the Providence!

Now the entire solar system was in view as I stood floating on the edge of it. The music of the spheres sang out—full of grandeur. And I saw the sun: faint but brighter than any star. The immensity of the solar system lay before me. After rejoicing, I turned and followed the three souls sent by God.

We flew to the outer edge of the solar system, where beyond the rim were mists. The mists became a wide band of clouds, mutely lighted from within. They shone eerily to my sight as we flew upward and into them. Now the clouds became a world of many different places.

I had a crystal clear and panoramic view of this world. It was a spectacle of horror unlike anything on earth—or even imagined. A montage of evil was all-encompassing. The inhabitants who existed here were both terrifying and ludicrous. The sights I witnessed astounded me. There were places upon places—very vile—as we went up through the mists of clouds. This is where the wicked of earth go after death, including all those who sinned and would not repent nor accept Jesus as their Lord and Savior. This is the Netherworld, the abode of the wicked dead (Matthew 25:41, 46).

And I observed carefully and write down here what I witnessed: Now as we traveled upward through the clouds, we came to a place of torment, and there I saw horrible man-like beings. They were monstrous humanoids—big-headed with tumors and warts covering their robust bodies. Their rubbery psoriasis red skin pulsated and twitched as if infested with worms. Though I could not smell or hear (for the impregnable sheath encapsulated my soul), they must have smelled atrocious, like putrefying flesh. Gross as evil can possibly be.

Snarling, saliva-sputum dripping, they bit their tongues. Their dark bulging eyes ferocious. Atop their grotesque head was curly brown-gray hair, and their bushy eyebrows pointed upward on a slant.

They were an ugly lot, indeed! They were mean-hearted and oppressing—animatedly the souls of man. The demon gave a quirk with a whip, flogging the damned souls who worked on weird machines. The poor, unfortunate sinners, who looked to be in the prime of life, dared not protest or rebel against these horrid sadistic fiends for fear of being whipped harder. But still they were policed and beaten all the more, much harder, until awful pain was seen on their faces (Mark 5:2–5).

I progressed upward into the eerily lit clouds, following close to my three guides. Through the mists came strange, lubricious beings. They pedaled on by, each with a creepy smile on their face. The demon's grimaces were disgusting but comical, as if amusing themselves with some perverted thought. How truly bizarre these entities were!

Now as we went through the Netherworld into different zones and regions, I found that there were many other kinds of demons—the ogres. Some stood together on hydrogen sulfide clouds and watched us as we flew upward and past them. Though they were ferocious, I was unafraid, for the hand of God protected us.

And the depraved, fallen angels became even more numerous and varied. They had mean, diabolical faces with scary, sardonic, twisted grins. The gargoyles' bodies were colored umber and were as large as several men. As we went further and further into hell, the beasts became even larger and more horrific.

Now as we advanced higher, there appeared to be more open spaces between the sulfuric hydrogen methane clouds so that many vile places could be seen. Each place was a cloud, and on each cloud could be seen the souls of man doing peculiar things. On one cloud, the soul of a fat man wearing a top hat, black coat, and tie sat on a chair next to a small round table. He ate fully, then vomited. He ate the vomit and threw it up again. He did this repeatedly in a sort of binge-purge sequence with his own puke—a most repulsive sight, indeed. Watching the obese cosmic bulimic was sickening as we flew up past him (2 Peter 2:22).

Another noxious cloud held two souls, a man and a woman. They fornicated continuously. They did it with a frenzy; their bodies convulsed, engulfing the cloud with their carnal lusts, never seeming to satisfy themselves. When they lived on earth, they hurt others by their filthy, disgusting adulterous behavior. So now, they will receive their justified punishment. This immoral existence went on and on (Leviticus 18:1–30; 2 Samuel 11:2–27; James 4:4).

And there were many of these chastisement clouds. Each cloud displayed its own nefarious idiosyncrasy. Each showed its own vice or particular sin.

The clouds did not move, but were stationary, unlike the clouds on earth, which move about and dissipate. The atmosphere in hell is rancid and foul, quite different from earth's. The air is thicker, but clear, absorbing and retaining light—much like the interior of a giant planet, such as Jupiter or Neptune.

And all around us in the bowels of hell were the guardians—horrendous but spectacular creatures who surveyed Satan's kingdom. Many had huge wings and flew, keeping order among the debased souls of man.

One monstrosity did not have to turn to look this way or that, for it had four heads, like a hideously mutated Ezekielian cherubim! The four dark obscene faces of this megabeast resembled that of a snarling vampire bat. Its upper jaws puckered, revealing its fangs. The ears were distorted for hearing, and the eight black soulless eyes seemed to pierce the surroundings for any signs of disobedience. The behemoth flew slowly and quietly. The colossal forty-foot brown wingspan stretched out, seldom moving as it glided along, guarding its sector. We continued our ascension, protected in the globe-like sheaths. The dragon was now beneath us, disappearing behind the mists of clouds (Ezekiel 1:6, 10-12; Daniel 7:6).

And we saw another Draco, equally massive, fly above us. This one was quite different but just as shocking and vile. Recoiled, I orientated myself to have a clear view through the octane fog, as we went upward. The dappled light increased substantially against the background. Looking toward the thousand-foot nimbus—precipice, the lower cloud column spread out, lending a real nice pristine view.

The scary monster-superbeast had two small reptilian-like heads and two massive silvery-gray wings. At a glance, this creature superficially resembled a flying reptile—a pteranodon. But its features were much exaggerated, especially its size. The two heads were similar, except that the toothless bill was much shorter and lacked the pteranodon's peculiar bony structure protruding from the back of its skull. The creature's wings were broad and leathery, moving gracefully, much as a manta ray looks when swimming. As we ascended higher, the beast disappeared into this cumulus landscape, where the places of torture and pain are.

Now as we passed through the Netherworld, we came to the center. This area had fewer clouds and was vast, plus it was very well lit. Even though I did not see inferno fire alluded to in Scripture, I assume these places do exist and would be the source of the light (Mark 9:43–50). This was a world within a world, farther then the eye could see, the expanse had ample enough space for the denizens who existed there. As we advanced ahead I noticed this realm was devoid of human souls or the menagerie of ogres from the lower dark labyrinth regions.

But then I witnessed what could best be described as a "great gathering." A horde of depraved dragons—millions—assembling and interacting with one another. And so I asked myself, "Is this one or that one Satan, or is this beast him?" For the prophet John described Lucifer as a seven-headed dragon (Revelation 12:39). And I saw them engaged in gargantuan mock battles with one another, also avid socializing, flying to and fro. One can imagine an Archangel coming down from heaven; slaying the dragons on our behalf. Even so, the place was not chaotic or helter-skelter; there was a high degree of order and purpose (Mark 9:43–46). It was well orchestrated.

As we traveled through the expanse, I became more amazed at what I saw—dominions, principalities, wicked thrones—truly an unimaginable world (Ephesians 6:12). At one point, a throng of swarming dragons, descended, rushing by. Some gave lewd faces—posturing and looking a bit annoyed that they had to go around us. While others ignored our presence altogether, keeping sight of their destination to the despicable evil underworld below.

Now as we advanced forth, I found that there were numerous species of guardians, the next more horrible than the last. I saw that some were small, and many were giants. The variety was somewhat mind-boggling, and to think that these cursed abominations were once holy angels of light. They were beautiful and wonderful to behold, before being cast out of heaven eons ago (Revelation 12:3).

Then we stopped for a moment, and the lead guide came over to me and began mouthing, mimicking the super beasts, trying to humor me. For I must have looked scared and bewildered, so then we continued to progress higher through the clouds, spying out many different regions, going wherever the Holy Spirit led us. I followed the three souls sent by Jesus, and I observed carefully—writing this down, stopping when they stopped, and then continuing when they continued. Wherever the Spirit led us, we went. And lo, where we went was indeed terrible.

We then came to a plateau, which was a vast expanse of cloud cover. It was millions of square miles made of sulfuric hydrogen—oily, dark, and foreboding. Looking ahead, I focused toward the faint horizon, but only saw mists spiraling upward into the fog. The souls stood by motionless, gasping with fear, as if in a trance, with a soft liquidy, flaming jet black cloudlet, below the knees, which acted like a vice holding down the person in place. They all appeared young, for the soul and spirit are ageless. The cumulus-precipice swelled out enormously, toward the horizon above the expanse. Here on the eery plateau, a multitude of people from every nation crowded together. Suffocating in nauseating vaporous ammonia smog, they were like Goya's ghosts, reenacting their vices, gnashing their teeth.

And the cold (the all-encompassing absolute zero) and lack of compassion prevailed throughout. I saw no one who was free. No one had any privacy. All were being brutalized and punished for their unrepentant sins—i.e., their murders, rapes, mockeries, other crimes. When they were alive, they did as they pleased, being selfish and narcissistic, not accepting Jesus as Lord and Savior. Now they are incarcerated on these nasty dreadful clouds, awaiting their eventual physical resurrection (2 Samuel 22:6; Mark 4:22; Galatians 5:19–21; Revelation 20:5, 13).

I was amazed and astonished by the Netherworld that our Lord Jesus had me witness. But suddenly I was caught away by the Spirit and led out of the clouds of hell and back into space. I followed my three guides, and we stopped and looked into the distance. I saw lights: rays of pure white light shining off the suns of God, with worlds remote and unknown. My soul rejoiced with exaltation to see heaven and the gates of heaven. Rainbows danced to the height of the celestial sphere. The powers of God shone in unison. Like poetry to my eyes, their light was grand, indeed! The grandness was as only the soul could comprehend (Job 38:7).

I wanted to go there but couldn't, for no one in hell could pass into heaven (Luke 16:26). I write this vision down to warn you of the horrors of hell, as pleading and a prayer from the wicked dead to Almighty God. Receive the forgiveness of Jesus Christ; take Holy Communion as you can. Pray to God, and seek his saving grace (Jonah 2:2; Luke 16:27–30).

What is recorded here is a confirmation of the Holy Scripture. It is a definitive description and should be taken literally (Matthew 10:28; Luke 16:19–31).

Blessed be God our Father, the Holy Spirit, and his Son, Jesus Christ, who made heaven and earth. May the Trinity's love be in mind and soul. Amen (Philemon 1:25).

Baptismal signet (known symbols). Three geometric forms comprise this signet. The equilateral triangle symbolizes the Triune Godhead—Father, Son, and Holy Spirit. The circle symbolizes the monotheistic nature of God. The square symbolizes the wholeness of God. We become a part of the family of God when we are baptized.

Regeneration

Chapter 4

The Cleansing, Vision of the Three Crosses, the Seal

Now, I continued to passionately receive the Holy Eucharist regularly, letting the Spirit of God open my mind. One night when I walked with two of my good friends, Joan and Suzanne, I gazed ahead at the dusky, dark horizon, and as I looked up, a spectacular light filled the sky (Acts 9:3).

Praising God, my soul was enkindled and leaped for joy. I began to breathe in the Holy Spirit, and grew heavy as if a burden were placed upon me. We walked very slowly, then stopped. I asked my friends to go on ahead without me. I continued to breathe hard, and when the Holy Ghost (the Paraclete) filled my body, smoke poured out of my mouth. The Spirit overwhelmed me with light! A strong acute energy surged through my body, causing me to fall down on my knees. I was regenerated; every cell was transformed, cleansed, and purified. I wept and moaned as my hands and feet began to hurt. The consecration of the Lord had come; the purge was intense (2 Chronicles 5:13, 14; Acts 9:5, 11:16; Revelation 15:8).

Now as the Spirit moved me to stand, heaven's light became more glorious. I stretched forth my arms, my palms facing the sky.

The virtue of Jesus flowed through my head, down to my feet, up through my back, past my shoulders, into my hands, and out of my fingers into the air (Isaiah 44:3; Luke 8:46).

Then the thunder of God resounded. As much movement shook the heavens, the moon turned red, like blood. Crying out in the Spirit, I asked our Father not to abandon me (Joel 2:31).

After this, I groaned, and the power of Jesus began to subside. I could hardly move or walk when my friends returned, so they helped me up to a small quiet room where I prayed next to a burning candle. And there a vision came from Jesus.

I found myself in a strange and faraway land. The landscape was surreal; it was like a Salvador Dali painting, very hilly. On one small rolling hill, I saw three crosses. I went to the knoll, looked up, and was immediately above and in front of the crosses. There was a man suffering on one and a dead man on the other, but no one was on the middle cross except blood, for this is the cross of Jesus and solemn martyrdom which every Christian must bear (John 21:18–19).

Following this vision, I went downstairs and, with my guitar, plucked the gentle pleasing sounds of harmonics, working as the Spirit moved me. I sang out the things my soul wished to convey. All that evening we enjoyed Christian fellowship with each other. At about midnight, we left, and a heralding Āve, like an eagle, flew overhead following us on our way.

The next day, a friend from church and I noticed that the Lord had breathed on my door, causing a *sigillum*, or seal, to appear. It resembled flattened icicles going sideways. Everyone could see the white zigzags on the door's right-hand side, by the hinges. When I touched it, I could feel a curious tingling sensation. On some days, the whole door would shine in a glowing whitish-blue (Exodus 12:17–13; Job 37:10).

And I rejoiced, for I had received a gift from God so precious, like a pearl, that I looked at it as often as I could (Ephesians 1:13, 4:30).

Chapter 5

The Sweet Fragrance, Children's Drawings, the Tree of Life

Moreover, for weeks after my personal Pentecost, I began to smell a sweet fragrance from heaven. I could not smell anything else—except the anointing. The over the moon perfume inundated my space. At times, the aroma of roses engulfed me, making the earth seem fresh again (Song of Solomon 2:13).

And I saw children's drawings on the sidewalk. They wrote the words *way* and *son* with colored chalk. There were dots, dashes, and arrows scrawled on the walkway, pointing to the Sun of Righteousness, our Lord Jesus Christ (Malachi 4:2, 5–6). And the Word came to me, and I received a symbolic vision in 1983.

In the spirit I stood and saw a tree. It had only one branch. With my left hand, I pointed at the branch, and it went limp and died. There was a second tree which also had one branch, and when I pointed at it, it, too, went limp and fell to the ground (Zechariah 4:3, 14; Revelation 11:4, 7). Then I looked on and saw a third tree with many branches and olive-green foliage. A chorus of life enveloped the tree; it was beautiful and wonderful, indeed. I didn't want the tree to perish, so I blessed it with my hand, making the sign of the cross.

And I prayed to Jesus, "In the name of the Father and of the Son and of the Holy Ghost." And as I did this, repeating the blessing three times, my right hand, which made the sign of the cross, began to get hot, and it lit up. The tree thrived and blossomed, for it was the tree of life—the resurrection (Genesis 2:9; Revelation 11:11, 22:14).

Chapter 6

The Gift of Tongues

Again, I felt the presence of our Lord Jesus Christ, and he gave me a message in a vision at night. During the spring of 1985, when I was thirty-three years old, I was praying alone at home in Oneonta when suddenly I became overwhelmed by the Holy Spirit and went into ecstasy. I felt a tingling sensation in my mouth, and suddenly my tongue became stiff, hard, and rolled. It began to vibrate uncontrollably, and sounds issued from my throat and vocal chords. With my mouth wide open and not moving, I began to speak in a language which I did not understand (Ezekiel 3:26, 24:27; Luke 1:19, 20, 64).

Now as I spoke in tongues, as the Holy Spirit moved me, I had this vision: I saw large golden letters, like symbols, move upward, as if it were a large scroll. The Empyrean writing was glorious and very beautiful, shining softly. I continued speaking rapidly in tongues as the message moved upward and out of my sight (Daniel 5:5–31). Then the Holy Spirit released me; the tingling sensation subsided, and my mouth felt normal again. The message from heaven also ended (Luke 1:62–64).

But when the scroll continued to move upward, I saw more writing. The message was in English, with the words shiny white.

And then I heard a voice. I heard a wise, kind, voice from heaven, narrate what was written on the scroll, as it slowly went up (Acts 8:29; Revelation 10:28).

The Holy Spirit confirmed the Acts of the Apostles, saying that what I had just experienced was the Gift of Tongues.

God will give the power to speak in any language he chooses so that the Christian can witness to anyone of a foreign tongue. This spiritual gift may be expressed during private prayer (1 Corinthians 14:2).

This is how the saints spoke during the day of Pentecost. They were all filled with the Holy Spirit and began to speak miraculously in other languages, not by their own volition—that is, by moving their mouth and tongue on their own, but by the power of God. Like visions, the Gift of Tongues is given in a very dramatic forceful way (Acts 2:2–8).

Moreover, there was conveyed to me other information and supernatural knowledge on God's narration. It related to the nature of the universe, quantum physics, and spiritual mysteries, which I did not understand. A super-intelligence spoke, which naturally overflowed because of God's divine splendor and infinite creativity (Daniel 12:4).

Star of David. The symbol of Israel.

The Mass Mind

Chapter 7

The Tempter, the Cult

Seven days had passed since my baptism of the Holy Spirit, and it was Independence Day, July 4th. I decided to leave the city and hike up a mountain. Several friends accompanied me. After enjoying the countryside, they left and went back to Buffalo. So I went on alone in order to meditate on God and his creation, but when I came to a high place on the mountain, I found that I was not alone. There was a tempter ready to tempt me (Matthew 4:1).

He said, "Come with me and see." So we went into the forest and came to a cottage. It was beautiful and magical, having an eerie glow all about it, and it appeared to be standing on air (Revelation 6:3).

He went into the cottage, but I stayed outside. As I stood there, I heard beautiful, euphoric music coming from inside. The enticing Vivaldi sounds filled the air. I was enchanted and curious, wanting to go inside. He came out, and perceiving my wonderment, said again, "Come with me and see," but I refused (1 Thessalonians 3:5).

Rebuffed, his cunning persuasion suddenly changed into one of frustration. All his eloquence vanished, and he became angry. He went away bitterly, driving off on his motorcycle.

Great clouds began to fill the night horizon. They were very close, and I could see the top, bottom, and sides of them. And then they lit up with fire, exploding and imploding from within. How stark and powerful they were, sending lightning bolts into the upper atmosphere. They moved slow and silent across the horizon, staying still and at times displayed their spectacular works. Then the fiery clouds came above me, causing my whole body to tremble in pain. I could hardly move; the angels played with fire all night.

The tempter came back and sighed, puckering his cheeks in a funny grimace. He told me he rides the same time every night because all of America drives and that if he didn't, he would become sick. I laughed and went off by myself, reading verses out of the Bible.

The next day came, and there was yearning in my heart to be alone and meditate on God the Father and his creations. Alas, the tempter was there to tempt me.

He began the day by cutting a patch of short grass with a noisy lawn mower. "Why do it?" I asked. He arrogantly replied, "To improve creation, and because all of America does it. If I stop, so will America, because the devil controls the ways of the world" (Luke 4:5, 6; John 12:31).

He said he liked the fact that God's plants and animals are being destroyed because of machines and roadways, that the earth is full of noise and pollution now. And that noisy polluters like jet skis, motorboats, snowmobiles, all-terrain vehicles, chainsaws, leaf blowers, give self-centered people their kicks at the expense of nature and wreck the peace and quiet, causing deafness and disease in children (John 5:21).

I responded by praising God, adding that every kind of plant and animal should be respected. I said that mankind should take care of the earth and have a deep regard for all life, because God made them (Genesis 1:20–25, 2:19).

He became somewhat crass and vulgar mocking what I said by saying, "Oh, we have a new avatar (incarnate saint) sitting here." He continued to talk about all the things he does and then boasted, "Everything I do, the world does also, like driving a motorcycle or car. It certainly has defiled creation now, hasn't it?" I said I know.

These forms of transportation are filthy polluters and wildlife die and many become extinct wherever roadways exist. And look what's become of God's beautiful creation! It's covered with garbage and solid cement! What a disgrace: technology run amok, incapable of supporting a viable ecosystem (Luke 4:5, 6).

And everything has to be in straight lines: bland and ugly. Rivers and creeks are turned into cemented ditches, and vast tracks of land into lifeless parking lots and lawns. And now we are being forced by the elite to look at huge windmill turbines and immense solar panel arrays covering the ground (Revelation 11:18).

He pointed out other aspects of the mass mind-world culture, such as its hedonistic nature and ubiquitous materialism (1 John 2:15–17).

Technology is the great earth destroyer, desecrating and using the land like a whoremonger. The mass mind destroys the earth for money, and the devil loves the decimation (Jeremiah 51:13; Hosea 1:2).

The Lord of creation has made intricate ecological systems: the arid deserts, tundras, and plains; the wetlands, swamps, and bogs; forests, jungles, and brush lands; seas, oceans, lakes, and ponds; the rivers, creeks, and streams. Let no one destroy these, for God shall destroy those who destroy the earth, thus wrote the prophet John (Revelation 11:18).

And I witnessed many things, remembering quite clearly, in sharp focus, so in addition, which I would like to relate here, a week earlier after my baptism and while I was with another person, I recall that we went to Delaware Park in Buffalo, New York, and saw some disturbing things pertaining to the world. And we came to the park.

We turned to our left and then to our right and witnessed many people worshiping man and machines. In this far-out scene, there were men and women—exhibitionists—with beautiful bodies clothed from head to foot in dark-brown nylon apparel.

They stood motionless, like living sculptures, posing in various odd positions. People gathered about, crowding each other, admiring and even touching their athletic bodies, and while they were being worshiped, we heard the deafening noise of car horns blast. Another crowd was worshipping the cars (Exodus 32:1–6; 1 Kings 12:28–30).

The weird scene gave me an eerie nauseating feeling. Like a pagan ritual, the scenario continued before us (Acts 17:23).

And our Father in heaven is getting angrier every day because people worship a strange new god, a god of technology, glorifying machines and bodies (Exodus 32:19–35; 1 Chronicles 5:25, 16:26).

Then the person whom I was with urged me to leave, and he grabbed me by the arm. As we fled, a precipitous wind picked up a large moving truck, setting it down in the middle of a field.

I recall that we came to Delaware Lake. As I looked on the clear cool water, three white doves appeared on the surface. They formed a triangle, symbolic of the blessed Trinity.

Because it was the day after my baptism of the Holy Spirit, I was very moved by this profound display of love from Jesus.

Then the tempter, whose name was Adam, said laughingly, "If ya need anything, just ask. I'll provide."

"No thanks. God provides all," I replied (Philippians 4:19).

Sunset went, and twilight fell, shrouding the mountain in quiet eventide. Then the tempter came back and said, "Come with me and see." For he wanted me to witness more of what he has done to the world. So we went back into the forest and came to the cottage. When I entered, I was engulfed by a place of filth and decadence.

I opened my eyes and witnessed the sin of abortion! It is a most grievous abomination, which only a brutal nation would allow. When I saw this, I became sick and quickly left.

The tempter ran after me, huffing and puffing like a lunatic, saying, "If ya need anything, just ask. I'll provide."

And I thought to myself how the world is full of violence, like in the days of Noah—the innocent are being slaughtered, the poor are hated, selfishness and horror are the new gods (Genesis 6:5, 11–13; Psalms 14:3).

Then the third day came, and the tempter had finally gone. I was elated, thinking I was alone to meditate on God and his work. But I was not alone and saw other things pertaining to the world.

And I walked about the woods and came to a field. I looked on and saw near a pond an old woman dressed in a long flowing robe, and in the spirit of evil Jezebel, she taught a group of women. The

Amazonian sirens sang and gathered together, worshipping a fake goddess and glorifying their bodies (1 Kings 16:31, 32; Revelation 2:20).

Then I turned away and hiked through the forest. I came to a large clearing. There I stayed several days, praying to God, reading Scripture, and enjoying nature.

In the morning, I met a group of people staying in a compound. I learned, after their proselytizing, that they believed in a fraudulent prophet and teacher, who wanted to unite all religions and races. These cultists denied Jesus as the Son of God and ridiculed the Christian faith. They tried to convince me of their false religion, but I proclaimed, "Jesus Christ shall govern the earth." They hated what I said and began to trouble me. But I held my peace, praising God (1 Peter 3:13, 14; 1 John 2:22–24; 2 John 1:7, 9).

The day passed, and the evening sky filled with a wonderful sparkling light directly overhead, like the scintillations of electricity dancing on air. I stood and watched in awe. My soul was overcome with joy. The wonder was a glorious sign from God our Father, and everyone looked up in amazement (Joel 2:30).

After this beautiful display of love, when the lights which had danced so grandly dimmed and faded, I turned around and faced the cult saying, "See what God can do? Your false prophet can do nothing except tell lies" (Deuteronomy 13:1–5; 1 Kings 18:20, 39; Ezekiel 13:1–23). With that, I came down from the mountain, amazed at what I had witnessed and thinking to myself how hard it is to emulate the Lord Jesus (3 John 1:11).

Chapter 8

Apparitions: The Blue Cross, the Phantasm

Now I became very orthodox in belief, reading Holy Scripture with a passion and letting the Spirit of God open my mind. The Lord desired to show me a personal revelation, so I was granted this powerful vision in 1985.

Again, I felt the strong presence of God, and his virtue filled my body, so much so, that my head began to burn with a terrific heat. Then the hand of the Lord came and, with his finger, pressed the middle of my forehead. And a blazing light burst forth from the anointing (Isaiah 6:1–8; Daniel 5:5).

Immediately, I was in ecstasy and saw an apparition: a huge blue Latin cross, which shone like a jewel and pulsated, floating about two meters off the ground, staying stationary in front of me. It was like the Martyrdom Cross I had seen earlier during my personal Pentecost, but this one was full of life and was quite animated.

Then a parade of light began to radiate exponentially in all directions from the cross. It became a blazing, splendid, bright white.

So brilliant was it—like a nova—that I thought I would go blind and die (Acts 9:3, 8, 9).

And then the cross suddenly vanished, and a phantasm appeared. A huge black serpent began to wrap itself around my feet and then the rest of my body. I wrestled with the snake and held its head tight, so that it couldn't envenomate with its fangs. It began to strangle the breath out of me by constricting harder, so much so, that I thought I would suffocate and perish. But then I prayed to Jesus to save me, calling out his holy name over and over, and the viper finally uncoiled and let go. The Holy Spirit caused me to speak in tongues as I came out of the vision (Genesis 3:1–5, 32:24–30).

And this is every Christian's spiritual battle. Let the Lord Jesus fight for us as it is only he who saves (Exodus 14:14, 25; Jude 24, 25).

Chapter 9

The Sign

At night, I had another symbolic vision. This time I was by a large lake or sea. A man and woman came up and professed the gifts of the Holy Spirit. The two evangelists wanted some sort of sign and proof that my visions were from God, (Deuteronomy 18:18–22; 1 John 4:1–3).

So I stooped down and gazed into the water. Suddenly, a whooshing sound was heard, and I saw something dark circling. Then a small fish leapt out of the water and clung to the top of my head. Another fish leapt out, and still another, until my whole head was covered with live fish (the fish is a known symbol for Christ and Christianity) (Matthew 4:18, 19; Luke 5:5, 6).

I got up and noticed that the Christians were amazed at the sign from Jesus. The prophet busters really liked the far-out vision and said, "See, this thing that has happened could have been written in the Bible."

I agreed, for God does things artfully as he always does, with signs and wonders (Matthew 17:27; John 21:3–6).

Blessed are those who read this Christian book and believe, for the Spirit of Jesus is the true spirit of prophecy (Revelation 19:10).

But for those who would criticize the Holy Spirit will suffer the dire consequences (Numbers 12:2-10; Amos 2:11–16; Mark 3:29).

For the Lord said to the prophet Joel: "And it shall come to pass afterward that I will pour out my Spirit upon all flesh, and your sons and daughters shall prophesy, your old men shall dream dreams, and your young men shall see visions."

And also, upon the servants and handmaidens in those days will I pour out my Spirit (Joel 2:28–29).

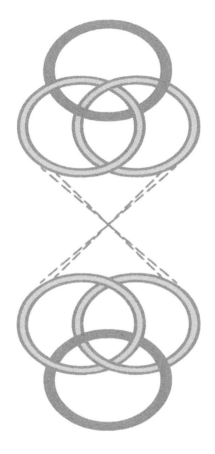

Creation symbol (composed by the author). The three intersecting rings on top represent the creation of heaven. The three interlocking rings on the bottom represents the creation of earth. The dashes are the creative force or energy of God. Like a reflection in water, the earth echoes heaven.

Creation

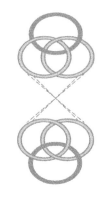

Chapter 10

The Beginning of Earth

My soul traversed through time, like light passing through air. I came and sat upon a small swirling cloud situated above other clouds which thundered below. The cumulonimbus and cirrus clouds spread thin and disappeared. I had an all encompassing view, seeing no moon or anything else but the cloud on which I sat (Revelation 4:1, 2).

How pleasant is the memory of the soul having traversed time! Sitting on the cloud, I curiously penetrated the air with the eyes of the Spirit, and I saw the earth. It was brown, green, blue, and white in all shades from dark to light. The hues were softened.

The memory began to unfold, like a gentle prayer plant which lowered her red-veined foliage by day.

The earth was kissed on its four sides. It then changed to a cold winter's cast, becoming white and bleached, losing all color. It was gnarled and rolled, like the ravaged stump of an old arthritic oak. A gentle wind, a zephyr, blew eastward and surrounded the cloud. There it stayed, rushing about my soul.

The memory began to unfold. With the calm of the gentle prayer plant, the earth revealed its mysteries.

As I went back further in time, the earth was transmuted. It changed once again. It now had no atmosphere, was as brown as wood, and convoluted like a brain. The terrain was rounded and shaped with valleys and hills. There were no oceans or any other bodies of water.

I looked with the eyes of the Spirit and witnessed an intense Stravinsky-like force come from heaven, and the earth fell apart, becoming like a cluster of atoms or electrical suns orbiting each other. Formless, it now became a mass of extreme force and energy. I entered deep into the fountain of time (Genesis 1:2). And I was awestruck when heaven opened and our Father, the great Creator, appeared. The God of Abraham and the Hebrews, the God of the Holy Apostles and all Christians, manifested himself to me.

Yahweh's effulgence was poetry to my eyes. His power and glory was all-encompassing. His long white hair surged forth like the mane of a horse, rope-like and wavy. It rushed up above, overhead, covered the length of his back, and disappeared. The rest of his body was unseen. His face was quite hairy, like the Amish or a musician. The long grayish-white beard flowed halfway down his chest. A white luminous apparel covered his glorious body. His manner was quite grandfatherly (Job 38:1; Daniel 7:9).

This was the appearance of our Creator's manifestation, and it was poetry to my eyes. The memory gave as the bee gives to the hive. The remembrance was very sweet, indeed.

I sat on the swirling cloud, with the zephyr rushing around me, and witnessed our Father. Like an artist, he stretched forth his arms and brushed with great bolts of lightning. He shaped the earth and moved back to examine it. Lightning proceeded out of his fingers and danced about the globe.

Then he appeared very angry. With his massive hands, he began to mold the earth once again. The earth took on the shape of an apple. There were rolling hills, valleys, great mountains, plains, and many other types of terrain. With his finger, he carved where the rivers would run and where the tremendous blue oceans would be.

Smoke issued up from the earth, for it was very hot indeed. This was caused by the magnificent bolts which came from the fingers of God.

Then our Father smiled, and I could see he was elated because of his new work, and he looked my way, smiling at me—a smile only the soul could comprehend (Matthew 5:8).

His eyes, which are the eyes of the wisest, stared into the earth. His love and Spirit fused into it, bringing up water, the elements, and life.

And the Holy Creator said, "It is good" (Genesis 1:31).

Now, the swirling cloud that I sat on lowered me down below the clouds onto the primeval earth. The eerie landscape was steamy. Much vapor mists spewed from the ground. Mammoth volcanoes erupted, exploding lava, debris, and billowing smoke into the dusky atmosphere. A dense fog shrouded the earth. The air and ground were very hot.

The Spirit of God fused his virtue into the land, bringing forth life abundant with grandeur. As I went, time went also. I could not tell how much time passed as I rode upon the cloud.

Megaflora (huge exotic plants)—fernlike and primitive—were everywhere. As I went, they became more varied. Some were tall. Some were stout. Some had long fronds, while others had short ones. They carpeted the land with their kind. And the Lord utilized every part of the jungle canopy. From the ground to the middle area and up to the tops displayed the web of life.

Then I came to a meandering river. Flying high above it, I went downstream. Huge dragonflies with wingspans of a meter or more across buzzed and hovered overhead. Colonies of giant Goliath frogs and salamanders as big as crocodiles hugged the riverbank. And there were countless varieties of plants, mosses, and lichens. I came to other rivers and lakes teeming with life. God filled them with strange armored fish, many flavors of lobsters, peculiar snails, turtles, eels, and periwinkles.

On the surface, water scorpions arched their tails as they swam. They would snap up insects and spiders with their claws and return underwater. They were portentous arthropods measuring fully five feet or more, a truly impressive animal of prey.

Countless varieties of giant centipedes, worms, and beetles of every color and design flourished in these misty forests of conifers. The flora and fauna took on every shape imaginable. For the Creator is diverse in thought. He created them out of his mind, and I was awestruck at the sight (Genesis 1:11, 20, 21, 24).

Then the Lord caused me to leave the river. I flew up above the ground on the cloud and the texture of the land changed once again. There were different kinds of plants, grasses, flowers, shrubs, and giant trees. Palms and hardwoods made up lush rain forests. Cypresses grew in steamy fens. Their roots, with conical knees, sucked up water. There were forests of giant sequoias and redwoods. They towered above me, displaying the Lord's genius and skill (Psalm 104:24).

The landscape changed. There were high-peaked mountains in the distance, as well as grassy plains and numerous exotic swamps. The sky became a bright blue, for the vaporous cloud no longer shrouded the earth.

Now as I went, time went also. And I saw fantastic animals— the great dinosaurs! And God made them fin-backed and horn-faced. He created the long-necked vegetarian sauropods and the foraging big-headed carnivores. There were varieties within varieties, species within species, groups within groups. The Lord made every shape imaginable. There were small ones, huge ones, two- and four-legged ones, some heavily armored. Others were ferocious, eating the flesh of other dinosaurs. A bizarre and diverse lot, they filled the earth with their kind and ruled it (Genesis 1:24, 25).

Riding on the swirling cloud, I watched as this scenario unfolded:

The colossal thunder lizards, *Brontosaurus*, and similar forms, paraded about in groups, stomping the ground with elephantine feet, eating soft leaves with their tiny grinding teeth. They foraged and peered over the treetops with their long snakelike necks on the alert for predators. At times they would stampede into the lake to escape the attacks of the king assassin, *Tyrannosaurus rex*, largest of the flesh-eating dinosaurs. With its jaws agape, monstrous head, and dagger-like teeth, the *Tyrannosaurus* was the most frightful of all God's inventions.

And the Lord created many other spectacular animals of prey—the very boisterous apex predators who specialized in controlling the numbers of giant herbivores. Some had terrible hands with huge claws for gouging out meat. Others were so small, they only ate insects and eggs.

Gazing down at the vast herds below, I saw whatever the Holy Spirit wanted me to witness and went wherever the Spirit wanted me to go. Whatever the Spirit wanted me to write about, I observed and pen here.

Praise God for his works, which are mind-boggling; his art fills the earth. Praise God for his mysteries and marvelous good taste (Psalm 98:1, 134:1-7; Revelation 19:5).

And I saw that some animals were given by God a bizarre array of armor, evident by the ornamentation of *Stegosaurus*. While others manifested impregnable spiked shells and looked like club-wielding giant armadillos or monstrous Galápagos tortoises. Many defended themselves well with sharp, formidable horns and raised crests. The greatest of these was the Picassian bull *Triceratops*, a giant beast with an enormous head and three sharp horns. The horns were used in mating rituals and as fine weapons against the swifter, more agile meat-eaters. These lived in herds, grazing like the American bison, stirring up dust on the open grasslands and plains of the Serengeti terrain.

Now most of the dinosaurs I saw were colored brown or dark gray, like African elephants and rhinoceros. The magnificent *Brontosaurus* was brown. They had a typical four-legged posture, with the head way up in the air, the serpentine tail dragging behind, nearly touching the ground.

And the Lord God made creatures with a complex social life and a high degree of intelligence. Many families of monogamous duck-billed dinosaurs inhabited swamps and rivers that were similar to the Amazon basin, raising their young near the water's edge. And there were unique animals. They were small, odd reptiles who were dressed like tropical flamboyant birds of paradise. Some ran to and fro on hind legs like a scrambling ostrich; many crept and crawled.

They foraged and roamed about the glade, like huge Komodo dragon monitor lizards.

Looking at the scene and then ahead into the distance, the humid tropical heat sweltered; clouds dissipated, merging with the cerulean blue line, the rounded upper portion of the thunderhead elongated out; their rain nourished the dense jungle canopy below.

For in the bogs and marshy savannahs, which reminded me of the beautiful Okefenokee Swamp, grew very strange plants that ate insects and small animals—even birds. Multicolored *Nepenthes* pitcher plants, jeweled, sparkling sundews and wild Venus flytraps inhabited these steamy moss-laden fens (Genesis 1:11, 12).

Now on the coast, the ultra-marine blue waters shimmered with reflected light. God constructed vast phosphorescent coral reefs which glistened, having psychedelic patterns in every hue. Cliffs embraced the shoreline and held exquisite waterfalls in their rocky crevices. They were hundreds of feet high, cascading down onto the boulders. Their spray hydrated the airborne midges and the raptors came to sip a drink.

Here, great flying reptiles, some with fantastic wingspans of thirty feet or more, glide above, preying on fish below in ancient seas. In the shallow waters swam giant marine turtles resembling the leatherbacks of today, but much larger. The huge flippers reached into the air, splashing down hard into the salty water. The giant shell obscured the sea. They were countless in number, flourishing under the hands of God.

And the Lord filled the oceans and seas with all manner of fish—big and small. For his pleasure he made them and it was quite amazing to my sight. And I saw that it was good, that it was really good (Genesis 1:21; Revelation 4:11). Praise God, all those who live on the earth; bless God omnipotent. Whatsoever the Lord wanted to make, the waters brought forth accordingly.

For there thrived tremendous forty-foot-long sea lizards. Fierce and fin-backed like a Chinese Nāga dragon, they hunted the open seas. While schools of dolphin-like reptiles flew in and out of the water, displaying their elegant form.

The Lord God created many life-forms. Out of his mind, he made them. How spectacular and bizarre his animals are! They turned the earth into a gigantic playground of eating, fighting, and mating.

Then time began to accelerate, and I went forward into the near distant future. Everything around me sped up at a hypervelocity. The animals dashed about, the sun circled above, and all the days merged together. On the cloud I sat and watched by an open field. And then time slowed down again.

Suddenly, great beings of light, giants, materialized before me. They began to kill the dinosaurs, throwing them about, as if in a game. The mass extinction was sudden and swift. Huge rotting piles of carcasses were everywhere, and I felt very sad because the sons of God annihilated the beasts from the face of the earth. Thus, the day of the dinosaurs had come to an end (Genesis 6:4; 1 Samuel 17:4).

But then I saw what was poetry to my eyes. And my heart rejoiced: There came out of the ground a whirling cloud composed of light and dust. This transformed into a fully grown giraffe! The animal stumbled forth like a newborn calf. After this, I saw another funnel cloud come up, and God created a mate. Thus began a new series of animals so that mankind can live on the earth safe and secure. These are humanity's living treasures and God's masterpieces (Genesis 2:19).

And the memory of earth's beginnings folded back, like a scroll being rolled up, and nothing else concerning earth's creation was revealed to me. This epic vision from our Lord Jesus, which I received on July 13, 1974, confirms the book of Genesis account of creation. It should be taken literally, not symbolically (Genesis 1:1–25).

Seal of Moses (composed by the author). The gold coiled serpent represents the great comission of Moses. First, a sign was needed, so God changed his rod into a snake (Exodus 4:3). Secondly, a healing was needed, so Moses made a brass serpent (Numbers 12:9). The triangular enclosure of the seal represents the divine nature of Moses's work.

Graces

Chapter 11

The Healing

N ow one night, during a vision, the Lord Jesus showed me one of my sins and said, "Either have this, or my body and blood. Which do you choose? You can't have both." So I tried to get rid of my sin (Titus 2:14).

A few years earlier, in 1983, about a week after my wedding, I developed an excruciating pain in my groin. The pain became even worse when I had relations with my wife. For a year and a half the chastisement continued unabated, day and night. And doctors could do nothing but wonder (Hebrews 2:10; 2 Corinthians 12:7).

I prayed daily to the Lord Jesus to be healed; visiting healing priests such as Father Di Orio, and others. I had also, the Laying on of Hands by members of my charismatic prayer group at Saint Mary's. God, then showed mercy and released me from my agonizing illness (Lamentations 3:26; Mark 5:25–34; James 5:11).

In the coming years, God blessed me with children. A year before the birth of my daughter Willow, I saw in a vision myself talking with her. She looked to be about five years old. Then a few years later, in 1988, my wife, Michele, became pregnant once again.

God said we would have a boy. We named him Joshua. Then again in the 1990s, an angel announced that I would again be a papa when I became fifty-four years old. When I became that age, my lovely granddaughter Shayla was born (Ruth 4:13).

Now, whenever I became ill, I would ask the priests for the Laying on of Hands. And I was healed a number of times throughout the years. Even tumors in my leg miraculously disappeared.

Then one day in 2000, a certain young priest prayed, and immediately I was healed of several illnesses at the same time. A year went by, and while I was working, lifting up a heavy roll of cotton watercolor paper, I broke my hand. So I went to him for a healing, but this time, he was doubtful that he could help. He began to give me a hard time, making me promise to see a doctor. I told him that I was healed of several things by his intercession, but he was stubborn and wouldn't listen. When he finally did the Laying on of Hands, as he began to pray, a foul stench, like human excrement, poured out of his mouth. I held my breath the whole time. The room reeked of his unbelief. Then he stopped, and I left the church (Ezekiel 4:12, 13; Mark 3:1, 3, 5, 6).

Needless to say, this time, because of his lack of faith, I was not healed. I had to go elsewhere to receive grace and to make my hand whole. But there are other reasons why the Lord may not heal an individual. I had a severe angina pain in the chest. A Pentecostal minister and I prayed for a healing, and we both felt the power of God fall upon us. But because of his disbelief, he said I had too much faith, I was not healed. And when I had my heart attack in 2008, I went to the hospital, where I eventually recovered (2 Chronicles 16:12, 13; James 5:14, 15).

Also, my diet was unhealthy, and the Lord did not heal me because I needed to change what I ate. And so my diet is healthier now, with good nutritious foods and exercise.

Moreover, the gifts of the Holy Spirit should never be polluted with intoxicants, such as alcohol or unprescribed drugs. Our flesh and blood is a new carbon based creation; the body is the temple for our soul.

Chapter 12

The Spring

With the coming of autumn, the trees became saturated with vivid Renoir color; the spirit of this season took command. And in my heart, a fire began to purge my mind. After receiving Holy Communion, I prayed that Christ would dip my soul in water, making me clean once again. Soon afterward, while I meditated and became quiescent, I stood by a deep spring and looked on. It was about the size of a small pond, approximately thirty by forty feet and bricked up with gray stone. On the surface of the water were dead fish and slimy algae, which made the spring reek. The whole place had a surreal atmosphere, like a Hieronymus Bosch landscape. It was peopled by the heathen and was very dark. This represented the world (1 Chronicles 11:17, 18; Colossians 2:8).

As I walked around the spring, an old hag laughed, distorting her face ludicrously, and said, "Don't ya slip now, ya hear." But I fell headfirst anyways and sank down to the bottom. This represented my sinful human nature (Jonah 2:5).

Then I began to swim upward, and as I did, the water became clear. A very loud commanding voice from heaven said, "Look down!"

So I looked down to the bottom of the pool and saw a big stopper preventing water from drawing out. The pool became fresh, like a mineral spring, quite different than before. But still I was frightened and held my breath for fear of drowning. So desperately did I swim upward and upward that I flew out of the baptismal spring clean and sinless (John 9:1–11; 2 Corinthians 12:9)!

Then the Holy Spirit said, "Awaken."

So like a jonquil breaking ground in the spring, my soul awoke. I felt calm and very clean, indeed. I knew the Lord Jesus had washed my sins away (2 Kings 5:14; John 4:14).

Chapter 13

Gift of the Christi Luminum

Now after receiving Holy Communion and numerous anointings from the Holy Spirit over many years, I received the Gift of the Christi Luminum in 1985 (Matthew 17:2). I prayed one night for the Christ light, and the Lord quickly responded by pouring out his radiant splendor from within. The blinding, dazzling light grew and grew more powerful with every second, consuming my whole body. My head became very hot from his glory. I could feel the rays in my fingers, like a burning laser as God's light went through them. I kept praying and worshipping God with all my might. But then the blazing light became too intense for me, so Jesus released his awesome power, and the Christi Luminum subsided (Mark 9:2, 3; Luke 9:29).

Now, for several years, I received the Gift of Christi Luminum often in my home, usually at night or sometimes in the afternoon during prayer. It seems to increase in strength and duration each time, and like with most visions, this happened while I was awake. But only after partaking in the Eucharist regularly and the Sacrament of Reconciliation does this charism manifest (1 John 3:2).

Jesus fully expressed this gift during his transfiguration. Moses, to a lesser extent, was seen shining with the Christ light. The bright illumination was not a secret one. Anyone could see the light shine from them. For mankind is the pinnacle of innovation. Our soul is the temple of God as the Lord taught (Exodus 34:29–35; Hebrews 3:3).

Moreover, in church, the Holy Spirit is also poured out with powerful anointings. This occurs during the Laying on of Hands and at the Reconciliation. It also happens when Holy Scripture is read or by witnessing to others the kingdom of God. When someone is hugged by a loved one, they can feel the other person's presence; with God it is the same. When he pours out his Holy Spirit upon some soul, he is actually hugging and loving them. And that person will feel the Lord's presence. I myself go into ecstasy and feel a wonderful transference of love from Jesus. A warmth goes through me—first, on top of my head—and then it passes thoughout my entire body until I am filled with the Holy Spirit. When this happens, I can feel the power and virtue of God radiating from me. Nothing feels better than this; it is true bliss. When Jesus healed the sick, he could feel the power and virtue leave his body (Luke 8:46).

There is one baptism taking three forms. One is with water, which is the baptism of Saint John, and we receive this when we are young. As we mature in the faith, the baptism of the Holy Ghost is given. This gives us our spiritual gifts or charisms (John 1:33; Acts 2:38; 1 John 5:6–8). And then the baptism of Jesus, which is with fire. This, as mentioned, is Christi Luminum. This prepares the Christian for the eventual supernatural body, which is like the eternal, glorious body of Jesus (Luke 3:16; 1 Corinthians 15:44–54; Romans 6:3–5; 1 John 2:25, 3:2).

Praise God for his wonderful presence and his many gifts (1 Peter 1:3, 4).

Chapter 14

The Noahian Rainbow, Inner City, Shekinah, Poltergeist

I n the gospels, we are taught of the gracious love Jesus expressed toward the poor. In the early 1980s, my wife and I lived simply in our humble abode, not having much. One day, a man from a Pentecostal church visited. He troubled me for being impoverished. This was wrong because he was a Christian given to hypocrisy. And besides, God fed Elijah, who had very little. And I gave thought to God's love for those in poverty and that the poor are loathed by this society (2 Chronicles 1:11; 1 Kings 17:2–6, 9–16; Matthew 6:19, 20). Howbeit that Jesus was at times homeless and that his ministry was supported by 'well to do' women.

Now, throughout the years, people maligned me, so when a priest hassled, I became livid, for they say in church, "Love the poor." And as I walked with my wife, Michele, I looked up to heaven and complained to Jesus about the priests' insensitivity (Deuteronomy 24:14, 15; James 2:5, 6).

Within minutes, the Lord's bow appeared in the sky. Then another huge magnificent rainbow formed and spread out above it. The immense double rainbow was so vast that it arched across the entire Oneontian Valley from one mountain to just over Franklin Mountain! The Noahian rainbow's colors were stark and vivid. We rejoiced to see this (Genesis 9:12–15; Esther 9:22).

Then the Word came, and God's Spirit lifted me up, taking me away to a large city, and I was set down in a neighborhood, where I saw the "angry young man" with no hope and full of despair. The neighborhood was like the one I grew up in—with my family in the 1950s and early 1960s. But now, the housing projects were dark and desolate, populated with gangs of violence (Proverbs 1:10, 11; Ezekiel 37:1).

In this symbolic vision, I encountered a group of young people, then I prayed, "Lord God, most powerful, give me the strength by your Spirit to defend myself." So by the power of God, I impressed the gang, who now let me by. A priest came and taught the black and Hispanic youths about Jesus and his wonderful teaching concerning brotherhood and nonviolence. For there is a need for missionaries to go into the inner cities and preach the Good News of the gospels to the poor (Judges 15:14; Matthew 10:7, 8, 11:5; 2 Timothy 4:7). Now, a lot is said about what we should do if we become victimized. Forgive, if they are sorry. But what becomes of the perpetrator of the hostile altercation? The Christians should be aware of the fact that they may be subject to some sort of provocation by family members, friends or by strangers. I witnessed Christians being verbally abused in public for no apparent reason. We bless the perpetrator but God does not ignore the trespass- there will be some sort of reckoning.

For in Scripture, both in the New and Old Testaments, God promises to punish those who persecute his followers. And one night in August, after prayer and meditation, I realized the truth in this promise from Jesus (Genesis 19:1–11; 2 Kings 6:18; Acts 9:1–9). Here is an example of the many times my life has been threatened and the glorious sign from God that followed.

Now, as I sat in a restaurant in Kenmore, New York, which is a suburb of Buffalo, three men came in and began to trouble me.

The bigots looked my way, and out of the blue mocked because I am meek and wear my hair long like Jesus (Psalm 37:11, 14).

But I was unafraid of their menacing, for I knew the Holy Spirit was with me. And that God was on my side. So I cursed them aloud, standing up for myself (2 Kings 2:23, 24; Acts 13:6–11).

They left angry and waited for me outside. However, a storm suddenly arose, driving them away. The storm continued as I made my way home, so I came quickly inside (Jonah 1:12).

The remarkable tempest became furious with a loud noise. Reverberating, it sounded as if angels were smashing together huge striking shields. Unbelievable intense lightning flashes continually fired up, and they lit the sky. I was amazed and awestruck for the angelic storm was unlike anything I had ever seen or heard.

As I watched the poetry in the tempest and felt the divine presence, the Shekinah, flashes of light from the storm, merged with a building across the way. Bright white triangles formed and were imprinted on its wall. Everyone could see their beauty. I praised and thanked God (Exodus 31:18; Hosea 6:5; Amos 1:7, 10; Revelation 11:5).

So shall the Almighty deal with the offenders of his people. It will be with fantastic force and marvelous judgment, for according to the Scripture, it would be better for him that a millstone were hung about his neck and he were cast into the sea than he should offend one of these little ones (Luke 17:2). For each member of the Christian Faith is like a precious pearl to the Lord—those receiving the Eucharist regularly or notable visionaries like Saint Bernadette.

Today classic paranormal activity seems to abound, afflicting many people. Throughout the New Testament, Jesus exorcized evil spirits and gave power to his Apostles to do likewise. The Christian can invoke the power of the Holy Spirit. In medieval paintings, men such as Saint Anthony, are accurately depicted surrounded by these spirits. The poltergeist would tempt or distract them, even while they prayed. During purification this is eliminated from the environment.

A few days passed, and I had visions concerning oppression, which I will relate further here. But this time, it was reminiscent of the paranormal. During the day, I saw something which reminded me of Saint Peter's vision.

The Lord opened my eyes, and I saw spirits of the material world, the spirits that oppress and cause diseases in men and women. The apparition was like an Edward Hicks menagerie of wild animals and reptiles, reminiscent of Saint Peter's and the prophet Ezekiel's visions. Their presence vexed my soul (Ezekiel 8:10; Matthew 12:22; Acts 10:10–16).

Then I came out, into the light. The Christ light began to fight the poltergeist, exorcising it until it was gone. So the whole place became bright and clear from the glory of God. Then my spirit, like a funnel cloud, entered through the top of my head (2 Chronicles 5:13–14; Ezekiel 2:1, 2, 10:4; Luke 10:20).

Again, the message here is to be unafraid and let Jesus purify that which is unclean (Mark 1:32).

As a conclusion for these experiences, I would like to paraphrase what Saint Paul wrote in Ephesians 6:12. He said it best when he wrote that we do not fight against flesh and blood but malicious spirits sent out into the world.

Jesus stated in the gospel of Saint Mark, chapter 16, verse 17, that the sign of the believer is to expel spirits, speak in tongues, heal the sick and be immune to any deadly thing. All this is achieved by saying his name. No other religion can make such a claim—that their lowly members, no matter who they are, can perform such super human feats. The Holy Spirit will not hold back but will give unimaginable gifts. For Jesus also stated that the miracles he did, will be ellipsed by his followers, even doing greater things witnessed (Revelation 11:3–12)! All these charisms will be joined together in a miraculous crescendo.

So every Christian, especially the clergy, to some degree, have these gifts. And during an overcast afternoon in August, 1985, I briefly encountered a malevalent specter, so I repeated the phrase "Stand in the light of Christ". He bragged that he had my friend, and I knew what he meant, because someone familiar became a poor alcoholic. This all began after I moved away and hadn't seen him for several years. Eventually he denounced God and our friendship. Had he sought fellowship in a good church, as I suggested, he might have become well (Mark 5:11-20; Luke 4:31-36).

But the alcohol made him weak, obstinate and vulnerable, even changing his personality-from meek and nice to nasty and mean. This is a good reason not to indulge oneself in drugs or alcohol and marijuana; for it muddles the mind. But one can rid themselves of anything occult or paranormal by using the Christ light.

So immediately when the specter heard "Stand in the light of Christ" and felt God's presence, he was exorcised and fled the room (Matthew 10:1; Luke 9:49,50).

Chapter 15

Vision of the Little Angel

Our Father created countless numbers of angels and spiritual beings. These he made in every size and shape imaginable. There are powerful archangels like Michael and messengers like Gabriel, who govern and give momentous messages from God. There are huge heavenly creatures called cherubims; they are winged and have four faces. These, the Lord rides on. And there are holy seraphims who stand before the enthroned Lord. But he also made small angels, and the Lord Jesus wanted me to see one. So one sunny afternoon in July, I went into a trance as I gazed at my favorite plant, a split-leaved Philodendron, and saw on her leaf a little angel (Isaiah 6:2–7; Ezekiel 1:5–14).

Appearing first were sparks and the emanation of a soft light. This formed into a scintillating crown of twelve tiny golden candles. From beneath appeared a face that had a smile that penetrated the heart. The angel's ethereal body, translucent and white, materialized slowly, and the body had wings folded on each side, clear and fragile like a dragonfly's wings. The robed garment, which covered the angel from head to toe, radiated a soft white light.

We neither talked nor made a sound, but I looked on, and the little angel looked back and smiled a smile only the soul could comprehend.

This is but one of the many kinds of angels and spiritual beings our Father had made eons ago. From his mind, he created them, and they are countless in number (Nehemiah 9:6).

War signet (composed by the author). The two crossed ancient swords represent war. The skeleton symbolizes death.

Apocalyptic Writings

Chapter 16

The Illuminated Cross, Destruction of the City, the Empyrean

Now during the night of September 17, 1974, I received a prophecy from God, a terrifying vision of the future, one of death and destruction. I felt the glory and power of God Almighty. A fire from the Holy Spirit inundated my body so that I was endowed with the prophetic charism from Jesus.

I looked and saw a spinning illuminated cross advancing and rising upward, casting off a soft white light shining this way and that. Like a radiant jewel, it was made from the brilliant Christ light and was quite beautiful, indeed. By the power of God, I also went upward, raptured, following the cross, and we traveled through the upper atmosphere, into the clouds, high above the earth.

There I was met by an angel of God clothed in a bright white cloud. His legs were invisible and appeared to be floating midair.

He was slightly above the surrounding clouds. His grayish-white hair and beard were cut short. And like Yahweh, he looked ancient and wise. The angel was full of love and kindness, treating me with respect (Ezekiel 37:1, 2; Revelation 4:1, 10:1).

He said nothing but motioned to me, so I followed him and the spinning illuminated cross. We flew together and went high above a large modern city. Then coming closer, I was able to see clearly crowds of people hurrying about, going here and there. A harried throng bustled feverishly in automobiles, seemingly countless in number (Ezekiel 11:1, 24).

Then we descended into the city and floated above the ground next to a highway. Suddenly, there was a most grievous sight. The city went mad with violence and paranoia. Cars began smashing into each other. There was mayhem and chaos. People got out of their vehicles, frenzied, cursing and going on a murderous rampage. Blood was spilled, covering the streets. Everywhere in the city, the vehement emotions erupted into predation. Thus, the hour of rage had begun (Nahum 3:1–7; Matthew 24:21).

And powerful winds began to whirl across the landscape. Huge billowing clouds having multiple funnels underneath appeared in the distance. Mega-tornadoes with vortices a mile or so across were everywhere. They crashed into bridges, buildings, businesses, homes until the entire city lay in ruins (Zephaniah 1:14–18).

And I felt a terrible sorrow when I saw this. But before I could grieve, the angel of God motioned to me, and I followed him and the spinning white cross high into space. I could hardly catch my breath as we flew hyperfast to other parts of the earth and over several cities also devastated.

After this, we went upward through the clouds and above the gigantic hurricane. I could see the top of the tornadoes below and the eye—the epic storm continued to destroy the cities. Now the holy cross was rotating ahead of me, reaching an unimaginable velocity, breaking the laws of physics, and going light speed. And I wondered where the Lord was taking me this time. We went through a vastness of clouds high above the horizontal plumes of smoke and debris, far into space.

Suddenly I was caught away by the Holy Spirit and found myself ascending heavenward into a vast vortex of luminous angels! Like monarch butterflies, their beautiful wings were multicolored with a delicate design. Each Burchfield wing touched the next in juxtaposition, curving about and forming the tunnel. The angels' radiance was poetry to my eyes.

The passageway known as Jacob's Ladder was immense. It was many miles wide and hundreds of miles long. I looked about me as I went through the vortex, and the whole place was wonderful beyond belief. Time seemed nonexistent as though in a forever time rift continuum, and I traveled far, ascending until I reached the end of Jacob's Ladder, and stood on the clouds of heaven (Genesis 28:12).

I looked and saw a veil of rainbows with colors of a certain spectrum. There was red to violet, and yellow to cerulean Van Gogh blue. They arched in triple bows around a celestial sphere. Smoke danced sinuously upward from burning incense which contain the prayers of the saints. Great stars with an entourage of worlds without end could be seen as well. Then suddenly, I was transferred into the Empyrean—the highest heaven—where a magnificent light shone. When I came near, tremendous lightning bolts flashed from the light and all about it. It formed an enormous pillar of cloud and mass of lightning, like an electromagnetic storm, continually sending out huge lightning bolts in all directions! This was the same glory cloud that filled the Lord's temple and guided the Israelites out into the wilderness. The same celestial splendor was seen above Jesus during his transfiguration (Exodus 40:34–38; Matthew 17:5).

As I watched the cauldron of fire from the Shekinah glory cloud, the spinning illuminated cross flew into the brilliant light, exploding with the thunder of God. I shook and trembled as the Lord's cross vanished from my sight (Exodus 24:15–18; Deuteronomy 4:11, 12; Revelation 10:3, 4).

Chapter 17

The Swarm, the Crash, Mega-Tsunami, the Āve

Now, during the eleventh hour, my breathing stopped, and my heart beat slowed as the Lord pulled my spirit from me. I felt paralyzed and could not move. The Lord began to cover my eyes, but I resisted. I prayed to see what was occurring in the room, and I witnessed a most extraordinary vision (Ezekiel 2:2).

I could see clearly in two different spaces, with my physical eyes as well as my spiritual eyes. I looked at my spirit, and I looked at my body. I was amazed at the phenomenon (1 Corinthians 15:44; Revelation 4:2).

And during bilocation, my spiritual body was clothed in a very colorful hooded sackcloth, belted with a golden-orange sash (Revelation 1:13, 11:3, 15:6).

Now as my spirit walked about the room, the atmosphere became intense with movement, and a mysterious Pentecostal wind rushed forth. Then suddenly, God began to create a swarm of bees!

Springing up they gushed out, like a water fountain, near a "new earth" signet that I made a year earlier in 1973. And the swarm coursed across the room, acting with one mind—given by God (Judges 14:8; Acts 2:2; Revelation 16:1).

My spirit led them out through a broken window, and they flew into a smoky elliptical cloud. The cloud was unique, for it was bright in the middle like a nova, shielded by black mists. I heard the thunder of God resound as the Messianic plague cloud was taken up (Exodus 10:12–15; Isaiah 7:18).

Immediately, my spirit entered into me. I began to breathe again and felt my heart beat much faster, returning to normal. Exhausted from the experience, I fell into a deep sleep (Ezekiel 2:2; Daniel 10:8, 9). The next morning, when I went out, I saw children throwing rocks up at a tree. I stopped the little boys when I realized they were throwing them at the swarm which was clustered on a branch. But a few remained decorating my windows with wax. Those who visited saw the honeycombs on my windows.

This pestilence will grow in strength and size, chastising the corrupt, the destroyers of earth in the last days, before the return of Christ (Exodus 23:28; Joshua 24:12; Revelation 11:6).

The thunder has sounded, but there is more to come (Revelation 10:3). The hand of Jesus carried me away, and in the Spirit, I received more solemn premonitions—one was financial ruin and the other a natural cataclysm. In the year 1979, I received these visions.

I found myself on Wall Street, the financial district in New York City. As I watched the stock brokers buying and selling securities, the whole place suddenly became chaotic and riotous. The market had crashed. It was so severe that those who were rich and well off found themselves poverty-stricken, begging. They became as poor and homeless like the ones they despised (Micah 6:12; Revelation 18:7–15).

And this will occur before the return of Christ. He will come with great power and glory, rewarding the underprivileged and meek—the saints.

In another vision and prophecy, I witnessed a terrible natural calamity. This time, I was taken to a large city on the ocean coast.

Everything was calm as I pondered from a distance. I looked on, waiting and wondering what might happen.

Suddenly, a rogue tidal wave thousands of feet high came up out of the turbulent sea. The mega-tsunami swept over the entire city, covering the buildings, homes, and businesses, laying waste and submerging the city underwater (Luke 21:25; Revelation 8:8–9).

Now as I reflected on the visions I was granted, I looked and saw an Āve gliding down from heaven. The angelic creature spoke loudly. He oriented himself by moving his wings in such a way as to stay overhead in the same place.

And I was amazed at the Āve's size. The fine spread of his wings was spectacular, perhaps twelve feet or more. They were silvery and very thick where they joined the head, tapering off thinly at the tips. He had a peculiar face, and I sensed a high degree of intelligence in the flying apparition (Isaiah 6:2–6).

Remarkably, the Āve continued his heraldic pose, staying in the same place—at the zenith for quite a while. He was looking at me with love. Then gliding downward and lifting up his massive wings, he ascended into heaven.

But three excited Āves continued with me during the time of the prophetic visions when the Lord showed me things face to face. They were seen by other Christians, like Ishmael. They disrupted a prayer meeting in Buffalo with their loud shrieks and would glide high above, circling like thunderbirds, ascending and descending, heralding directly overhead wherever I went (Luke 17:37). Praise God, for soon Jesus will return to the earth with his saints and vast myriad of angels. Everyone will see them, the corrupt and those that are uncorrupt, and a new life will flourish on earth.

Chapter 18

The Cathedral,
the Zechariahan Mirror

And in the year 1985, the Lord revealed this vision full of vivid symbolism: I attended mass regularly, receiving Holy Communion and the Sacrament of Reconciliation often, abstaining from the indulgences of this world and fasting (Ezra 8:23).

In the vision, however, I found myself in a huge Cathedral. When I looked, I saw many priests and bishops walking in line to the back of the church. As I was watching them from the side hallway, they came up from the front again toward the altar. Then I witnessed a very strange thing: they all turned into women, and the whole place erupted with unrestrained revelry.

Then suddenly, a flying oval mirror approached and suspended in midair, floating silently in front of me. The big Zechariahan mirror reflected like soft rippling water. An ornate frame wrapped around the mirror in antique floral fashion. Then a young lady's face emerged from the silvery glass. She had a joyful nice loving smile.

Her long brown wavy hair encircled the inside of the mirror's portal interior border. As I gazed at her, transfixed, she suddenly vanished. Then a monk's face filled the gateway, but he too disappeared only to be replaced by a priest. Their reflections were as though they were in water. They were pure and wavy, rippling (Zechariah 5:1, 2).

And I saw the saints of the church throughout the ages; Saint Francis and others appeared in the Zechariahan mirror. These people dedicated their lives to Jesus and are now rewarded in paradise. They love God and obey his commandments. My witness was of the souls of both men and women who contribute to the church (Revelation 6:9, 20:4).

Then I saw the beautiful young woman Saint Maria smiling again, and the vision faded.

Chapter 19

Judgment of New York City

A gain, Jesus took me away; and in 1997, I was shown a dire prophecy of doom. I looked on and found myself in Central Park, on Manhattan Island. I couldn't see the buildings, for there was a dark, smoky cloud covering the entire area. Plumes of debris mingled with paper flying about filled the air.

And I looked up at the cloud, wondering what caused it. Suddenly the cloud dissipated, and I could clearly see the buildings. I rose up in the air. Now being on the side, I had a horizontal view of the entire city and its skyscrapers. For a moment, everything was quiet and still.

Then lo, a clear, supersonic wind began to push against the buildings with great force. The wind became so strong (like a Jericho blast or nuclear shockwave) that it began to bend the skyscrapers over, breaking them in half like twigs. The buildings crashed down all around me. Glass, bricks, and mortar were falling, shattering to pieces. Smoke, blood, and death remained. I wanted to stop the dire premonition but could not (Joshua 6:20; Jonah 1:4, 3:4).

New York City, the greatest city on earth, was judged and thrown down like Babylon. And the world will mourn her passing. Millions lived and worked there. No more will we hear her music or see her art, for within minutes she will be annihilated (Isaiah 21:9; Revelation 18:1–24).

Chapter 20

Leaders of This World, the Armada, the Anvil, Plague

Now while I was with a Christian friend Suzanne, the Lord opened both our eyes, and we saw the leaders of this world. Their aspect became as the fiends of Abaddon, all ugly and heartless. Then I saw the Infidel, the wicked, and they became even more wicked. But the followers of Jesus will shine with the light of Christ and will become beautiful with love and peace. They will be the *new leaders*. This, the prophet Daniel predicted (Daniel 12:3; Ecclesiastes 3:17, 18; Galatians 5:22, 23; 1 John 5:19).

Praise God, for Jesus will return to the earth and govern it.

After this, while outside, the prophetic chrism became strong so that it overwhelmed both of us. The Lord once again opened our minds, and as we gazed up, regarding the western horizon, there came huge, spectacular air machines pushing northward. Like a blitzkrieg, we first saw one, then seven, then twelve, and then many more, until the entire sky was filled with them (Numbers 11:25–30).

We watched them advance obliquely upward. They were one next to the other, the gigantic verdant wings almost touching as in a procession. The armada looked quite unearthly, for they were ghostly phantom bombers holding weapons of mass destruction. I felt like we were in the thick of the fray when the Armageddon crafts roared thunderously overhead, for they were going to a future world war (Revelation 16:12–16).

After this, a month later, the Lord Jesus again opened my mind. I saw a raven flying overhead, heralding as it followed me to a brook. I felt a small wind rush by, a zephyr, and the air became perfumed with the scent of roses. On July 25, 1974, the Almighty God had me witness something.

All of nature became fixed in time so that nothing moved, except myself and the excited bird. As I came to the brook, the raven vanished, and I saw on the other side peculiar billowing clouds of smoke. As the ashes settled, a plague appeared. It was created out of the ashes that poured out of the billowing clouds. And flies covered the whole area—the ground, the plants, and the trees (Exodus 8:21; Haggai 2:1; Revelation 9:1–3).

Then I ran and went into a field, hearing above me the powerful and deafening blows of a judge's hammer hitting an anvil, for the Lord God Almighty was judging the world. His just wrath caused the creation of the chastisement, and he will punish by the awesome power of nature as he has done many times before (Revelation 11:6).

Chapter 21

Ecological Cataclysm, Earthquake Event, Sign of Skorpios and Equus

In another symbolic occurrence, I was shown what will happen when technology collapses, and I saw mayhem! Vehemently, the people cursed and raged terribly, for the world blindly follows science, with its false teachings, like the theory of evolution, insulting God our Father, who created all life (2 Thessalonians 2:8, 9).

The Lord then opened my eyes, and I saw a sign of impending ecological disaster that will decimate many of the earth's forests. I witnessed a terrible blight, killing the leaves of the trees. In vision, the forests were gone. Nothing remained except smoldering ash (Revelation 8:7).

So let us glorify the true God of nature, the blessed Trinity, who created heaven, earth, and the celestial bodies. Let us care for the wildlife entrusted to us since the time of Adam and Eve.

Then in 2010, I heard a thunderous voice from heaven, which prophesied: "There will be a major earthquake event!" Earlier I had felt a great trembling. In vision, it was the power of a major quake. As I stood holding on in the doorway and looking on, the terra firma suddenly opened up (2 Samuel 22:8; Habakkuk 3:5).

Now in 1974 while outside, I witnessed wonders in heaven. The Lord Jesus opened my eyes, and I saw an impetuous storm approach, and lo, a derecho wind, with a throng of Skorpios, punctuated the gray sky. Like a blitzkrieg, their arched tails snapped forward like whips. They traveled straight, moving their bodies as if surveying the earth. Their claws and antennae engulfed the clouds. With one mind, they advanced, like an army of soldiers who were kill shocked. When the sign of Skorpios dissipated, a discomforting quiet filled the air (1 Kings 12:11, 14; Revelation 9:1–11).

Then another sign and wonder appeared, and the forces of heaven broke loose again! I looked up and saw a great white horse without a rider, for the rider had been sent down to the earth. Then the enormous Equus moved upright and stood on his hind legs on a massive thundercloud. With his head tilted back, his white mane cascaded over the shoulders down his back. His muscled body, which was as massive as the thunder cap he stood upon, seemed incredibly strong but weightless.

I was mesmerized by the Biblical horse, which then went off into heaven (Habakkuk 1:8; Zechariah 6:3–6; Revelation 6:2).

Chapter 22

Night Vision: The Throng, Metamorphosis

N ow winter's cast colored the ground with all manner of shadows, and the chill cold weather clasped the season. White, everything was in the shade of white—the aspect of God, the symbol of Good.

Thus, I mused over this and over that, going wherever my mind went. Then on the wintry night of February, I received a personal revelation from Jesus.

I looked on with crystal clarity and saw myself on a street near a crowd of very angry people. Their hardness was terrifying, full of strife. As I watched myself amid the crowd, I noticed that I looked much younger and felt rejuvenated, I wore my hair short and did not have a beard (Jeremiah 1:8; Ezekiel 2:6; Galatians 1:10).

Then in the precognitive night vision, I saw the excited throng advancing, running after me. The power of the Lord came on me very forcefully, so I was able to miraculously leap a whole cityblock.

As I was carried off, they reached up to grab, cursing with vulgar obscenities. I came down on the street again and turned to see the crowd coming closer (Obadiah 1:2).

Then I witnessed a most remarkable thing: I saw myself turn into light! The metamorphosis caused my whole body to shine; my flesh became translucent and bright (Exodus 34:29–35).

The crowd came nearer, and as they approached, God's Spirit lifted me, and I flew up in the air. As I was levitating, I looked down and saw that they continued to curse, raising their fists high above them (1 Chronicles 16:22; Revelation 11:3–12).

I went on my way, witnessing other things, writing diligently of the woe and mourning for and by the things to come. Then when the Word came, I found myself living in Jerusalem.

And I gave thought to the things shown to me and write them down here. In vision, I came between the heavens and the earth; above an immense lake, singing and praising God with exaltation. I raised my hands in prayerful Bennediction; an invocation of God's divine blessings.

Then one night in June, a Christian friend-David, had a word of knowledge and he said, "As I lay in bed, a brightness came over me and in a vision I saw you being slain in the spirit, (which is a known charismatic gift)". And we continued to enjoy Christian fellowship; worshiping and studying the gospel with a passion and receiving Holy Communion regularly.

Then nine years later, when my wife left town to visit relatives, I was alone and prayed next to a candle. The Spirit of God came down onto the flame; the Pentecostal aura suddenly flared, shooting up, almost to the ceiling! I was taken aback and went into ecstacy filled with the Holy Ghost.

And then heaven opened; a cosmic cloud spread out and a royal thunderbird with healing in his wings, came forth out of the vessel of light (Zecharich 5:9). The holy apparition was heralding, coming above me, all the while, my hands burned, raying out with the Christ light. And while I was being slain in the spirit, my hands began to hurt, as if wounds were opening up. But I became frightened from the emerging stigmata; from the excruciating pain (Romans 6:3-6).

So the spiritual crucifixion ended and my hands cooled, returning to normal. Thus the holy vessel was translated into heaven vanishing from my sight.

But even to this day, I sometimes feel a physical manifestation, an escthetic piercing sensation in the middle of my palms; a sign to an unbelieving world. For in the latter days, we will receive his wounds and be sealed unto God (Galatians 12:20).

Chapter 23

War

Now the apocalyptic vision and prophecy from Jesus Christ unfolded, like a drawing scroll being rolled out. It was very articulate in its expression, casting future events before me. On the wintry night of January 23, 1976, I saw a cross, and it spun as it rose above me. Like the scintillations of a diamond, its soft rays were spinning off this way and that. I began to rise also, for I was raptured. I followed the cross wherever it went. I stopped when it stopped; I rose when it rose. And I followed the spinning, shining cross high into space. I could see the whole earth and its beauty. Like a musical sphere, it sang out with life. As I watched the good earth, praising God, our Creator, the spinning white cross thundered and disappeared. I came near and had a clear panoramic view of the earth. Clouds that drifted above suddenly vanished. The earth unfolded and was laid flat so that it resembled a huge map (Ezekiel 11:1, 24).

Below me was Northern Africa and the Middle East. A great meandering river bolted like lightning throughout the arid land. My view was unobstructed across Europe and Russia up into the north.

I could see the dark indigo blue of the Mediterranean, the light red-brown of the deserts and mountains, with green flourishing here and there. The earth sang out with life.

Now as I looked at the Nile River below me, swords appeared. They were antique, polished and white, for the hostility was ancient. They were laid across the river on both sides. Side by side, they were placed. A sword pointed west, while a sword pointed east, and they formed a row up and down the river. All was still as I watched and waited.

Suddenly, a sword flew a short distance and struck the earth. When it hit, billowing clouds of smoke formed into a mushroom cloud. As soon as this happened, another sharp sword flew eastward, crossing over the Red Sea, into the heart of the attacking country. The retaliation became fierce. Like a blitzkrieg, this sword flew, and that sword flew, and deadly mushroom clouds formed all over Egypt and part of the Middle East.

I regarded the frightening scenario for a moment, and as I watched, many more rows of swords began to appear along a wide path northward. They were placed along the borders of Iran, Iraq, Syria, Jordan, and throughout the Holy Land. But as soon as they appeared, they would fly this way and that, covering the land with nuclear explosions. Saudi Arabia was on fire, and all of the Middle East was now devastated (Ezekiel 30:4–8, 11, 38:21).

Rachel again wept for her children, Israel. Then the horrid war escalated, spreading northward into Greece and the Baltics. Swords were juxtaposed on the borders of many countries throughout Europe: Italy, Spain, Czechoslovakia, Poland, Hungary, Germany, France, Britain, the Soviet Union, and up into the north (Jeremiah 31:15; Matthew 24:7).

Swords appeared. They flew and struck, flew and struck, flew and struck, so much so, I could hardly discern Europe anymore, for so many mushroom clouds obscured my view.

Billowing clouds were full of the dead. Hell consumed all the living. Terra firma became a specter of a nuclear holocaust.

I could see all of the earth, from one end to the other—the Arctic to the Antarctic, the Orient and the Occident—and sorrow fell on my soul.

Then the earth folded back on itself and became like before. But as I looked at the Arctic regions, a mysterious white began to spread down on the earth. It was like a sheet of light. It covered much of the Northern Hemisphere, including my own country, America.

Those powers—such as the United States and Russia, who contributed weapons and money—are responsible for this war. God Almighty shall humble those arrogant nations and destroy them (Amos 1:11–12; Luke 21:20–24; Revelation 16:14–16). And I pray for those who are decent that they may be lifted off the earth or die suddenly before the nuclear war. Otherwise, death will slowly fade and consume them (Zechariah 14:12).

But Jesus the Messiah, with the saints and prophets, will return to the earth, healing and restoring it once again (Jude 1:14). Praise God our Father, his Son Jesus, and the Holy Spirit. Amen.

Seven principles (known symbols combined by the author). This is a combination of symbols:

1. The dove represents the Holy Spirit.
2. The seven-branched candelabra symbolizes perfection.
3. The inverted cross symbolizes martyrdom. (Saint Peter's cross) (John 21:18, 19; 2 Peter 1:14).
4. Alpha and Omega represent beginning and end (Jesus Christ).
5. The three burning flames symbolize purification.
6. The Christian symbol (upper left) represents faith.
7. The middle symbol is four triangles, which represents the Father.

About the Author

Multimedia artist Curtis D. Yax was born in 1952 in Buffalo and now resides in Oneonta, New York, with his family. Self-taught in art, music, and writing, he employs all three in Christian prophecy. He has exhibited in museums, such as the Albright-Knox Art Gallery and the Memorial Art Gallery in Rochester, New York. Also, he has shown internationally in Paris, France, and has won awards for his work. He has written newspaper articles and contributed to CPN,—a botanical magazine, writing numerous articles on the cultivation of carnivorous plants. Curtis is currently working on a children's book and is collaborating on a narration version for *The Book of Visions* using his own musical compositions.

CPSIA information can be obtained
at www.ICGtesting.com
Printed in the USA
LVHW011946240623
750446LV00009B/118